FIVE FINGER PIANO

5 CHILDREN'S FAVORITES

WITHDRAWN

CONTENTS

ISBN 0-634-01756-X

HAL•LEONARD®
CORPORATION

7777 W. BLUEMOUND RD. P.O. BOX 13819 MILWAUKEE, WI 53213

Visit Hal Leonard Online at
www.halleonard.com

America
(My Country 'Tis of Thee)

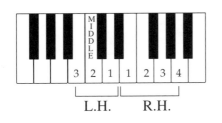

L.H.   R.H.

Words by Samuel Francis Smith
Traditional Music

Moderately

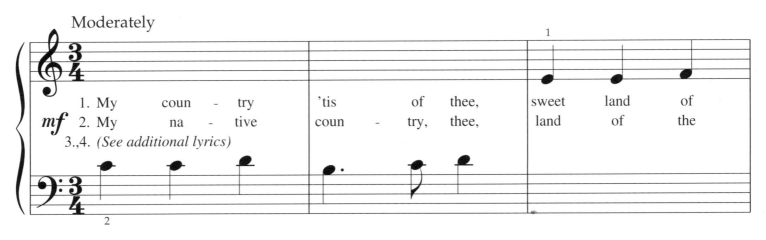

1. My country 'tis of thee, sweet land of
2. My native country, thee, land of of the
3.,4. (See additional lyrics)

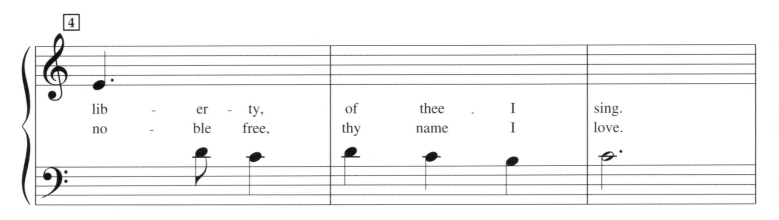

lib - er - ty, of thee . I sing.
no - ble free, thy name I love.

Duet Part (Student plays one octave higher than written.)

Moderately

Land where my fa - thers died! Land of the
I love thy rocks and rills, thy woods and

Pil - grim's pride! From ev - 'ry ___ moun - tain side,
tem - pled hills. My heart ___ with ___ rap - ture thrills

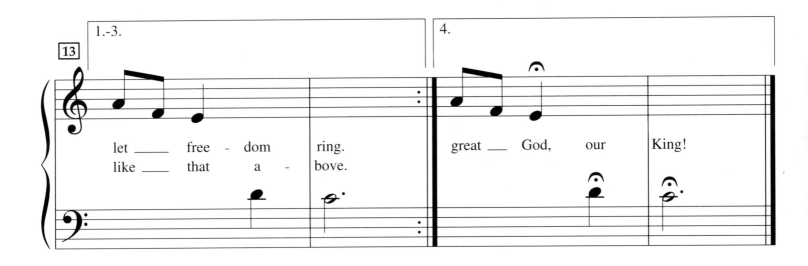

Additional Lyrics

3. Let music swell the breeze
   And ring from all the trees
   Sweet freedom's song.
   Let mortal tongues awake;
   Let all that breathe partake;
   Let rocks their silence break,
   The sound prolong.

4. Our father's God, to Thee
   Author of liberty,
   To Thee we sing.
   Long may our land be bright
   With freedom's holy light;
   Protect us by Thy might,
   Great God, our King!

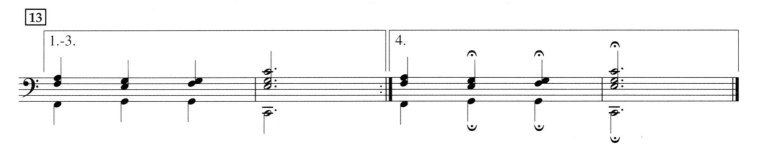

For He's a Jolly Good Fellow

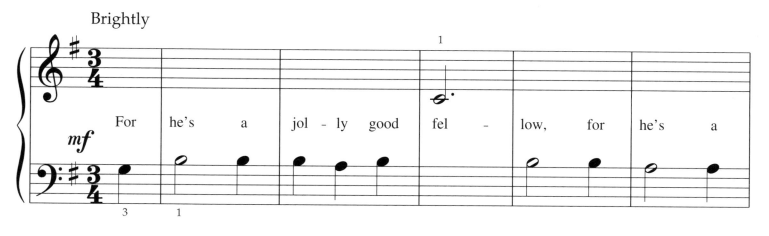

Traditional English Song

Brightly

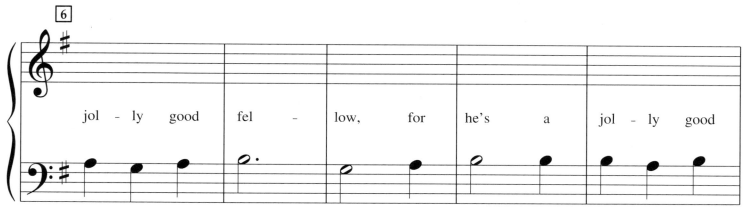

For he's a jol - ly good fel - low, for he's a jol - ly good fel - low, for he's a jol - ly good

Duet Part (Student plays one octave higher than written.)

Brightly

fel - low, which no - bod - y can de - ny. _____

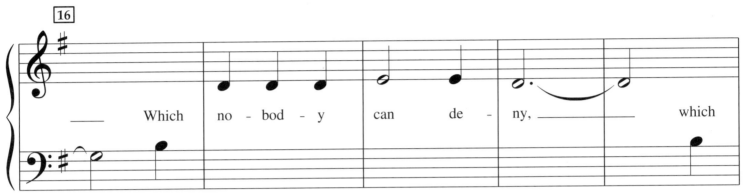

_____ Which no - bod - y can de - ny, _____ which

no - bod - y can de - ny. _____ For he's a

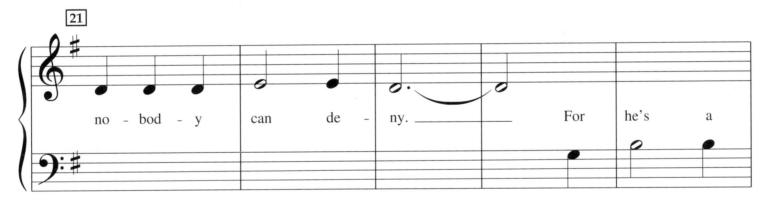

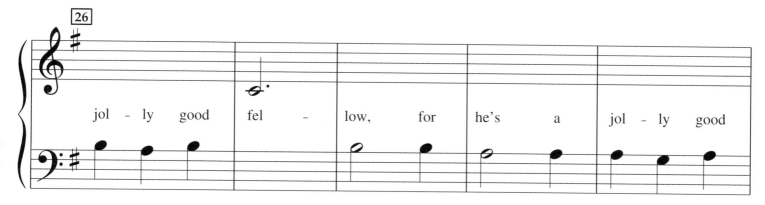

jol - ly good fel - low, for he's a jol - ly good

fel - low, for he's a jol - ly good fel -

low, which no - bod - y can de - ny. _____

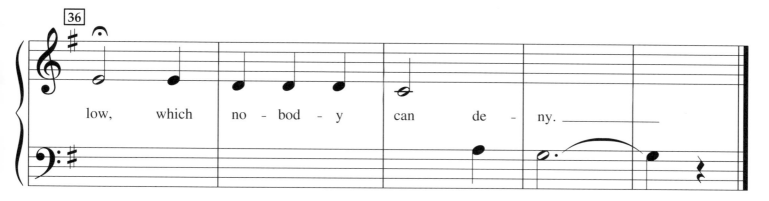

The Bear Went Over the Mountain

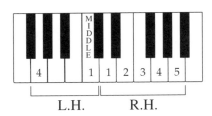

Traditional American Folksong

Brightly

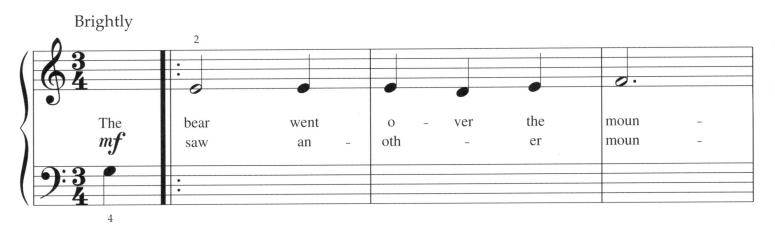

The bear went o - ver the moun -
saw an - oth - er moun -

tain, the bear went o - ver the moun -
tain, he saw an - oth - er moun -

Duet Part (Student plays one octave higher than written.)

Brightly

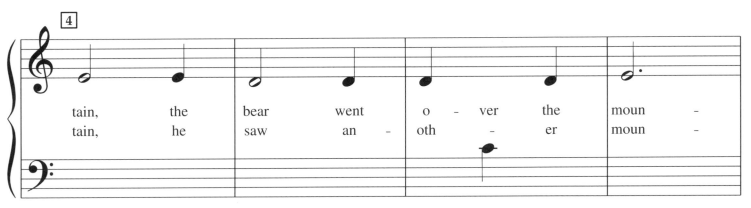

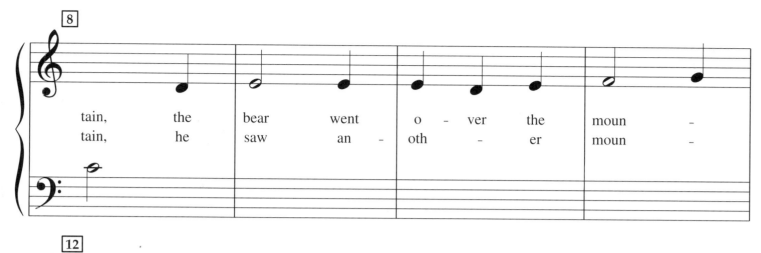

tain, the bear went o - ver the moun -
tain, he saw an - oth - er moun -

tain to see what he could
tain and that's what he could

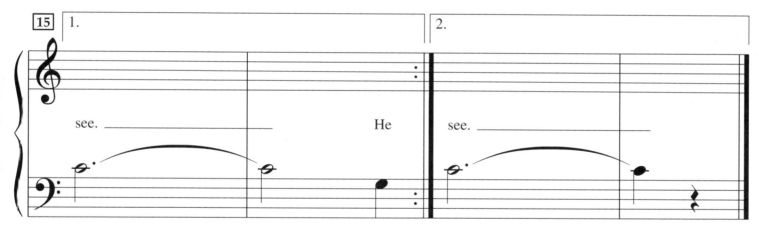

1. see. _____ He

2. see. _____

Goodbye, Old Paint

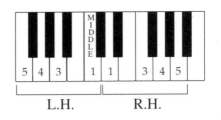

Western American Cowboy Song

Gently and flowing

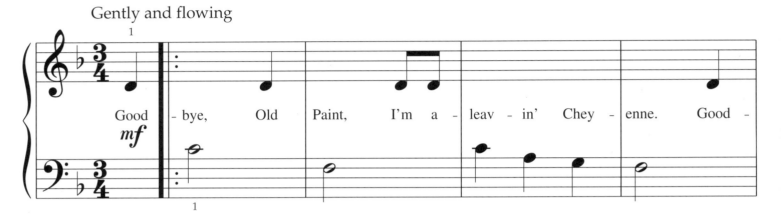

Good-bye, Old Paint, I'm a-leav-in' Chey-enne. Good-bye, Old Paint, I'm a-leav-in' Chey-enne.

Duet Part (Student plays one octave higher than written.)

Gently and flowing

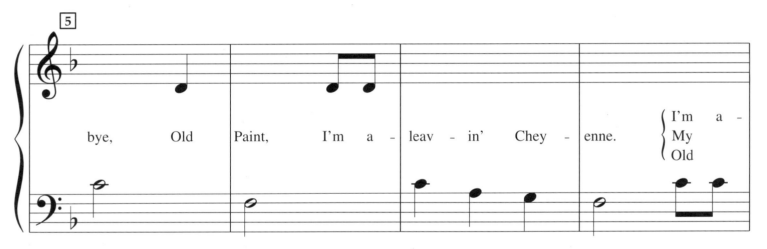

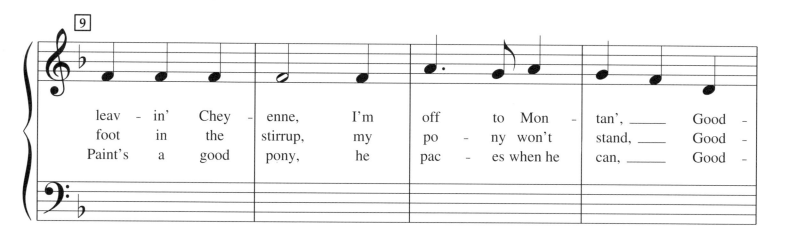

leav - in' Chey - enne, I'm off to Mon - tan', _____ Good -
foot in the stirrup, my po - ny won't stand, _____ Good -
Paint's a good pony, he pac - es when he can, _____ Good -

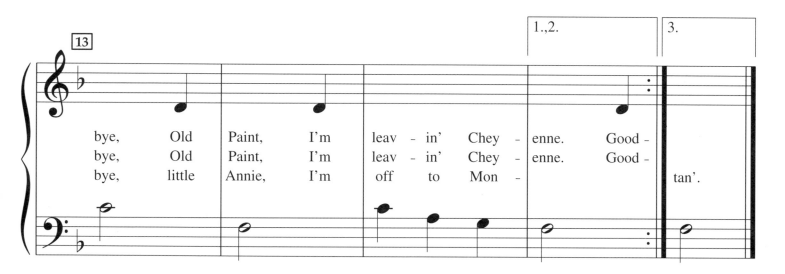

1.,2.   **3.**

bye, Old Paint, I'm leav - in' Chey - enne. Good -
bye, Old Paint, I'm leav - in' Chey - enne. Good -
bye, little Annie, I'm off to Mon - tan'.

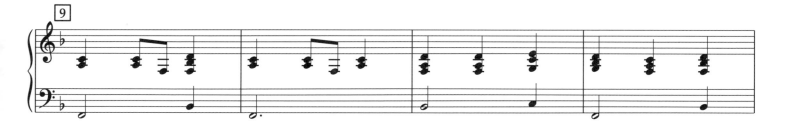

1.,2.   **3.**

Grandfather's Clock

Words and Music by
Henry Clay Work

Duet Part (Student plays one octave higher than written.)

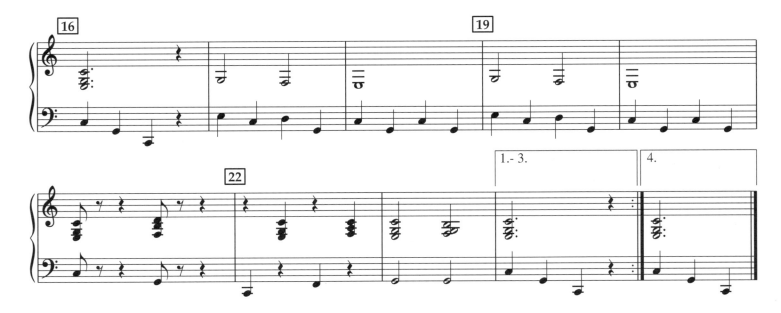

On Top of Old Smoky

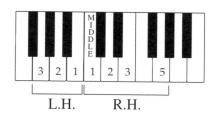

Kentucky Mountain Folksong

Moderately slow

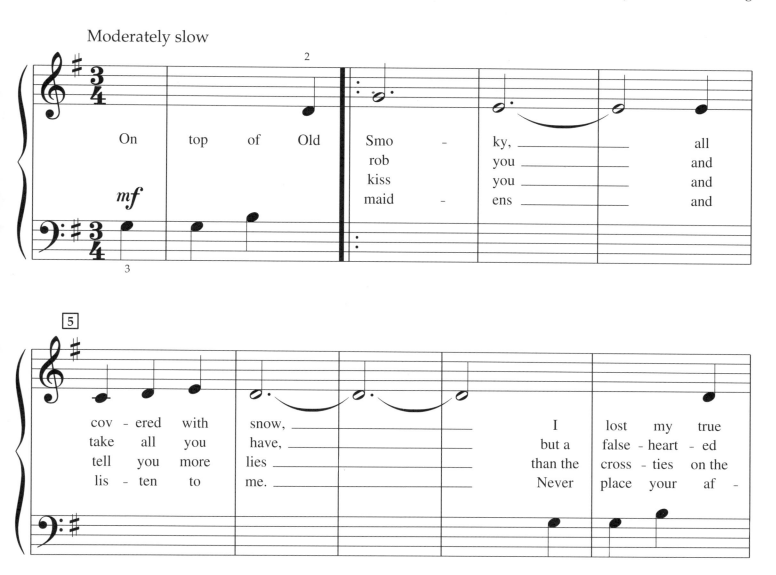

On top of Old Smo - ky, _____ all
rob you _____ and
kiss you _____ and
maid - ens _____ and

cov - ered with snow, _____ I lost my true
take all you have, _____ but a false - heart - ed
tell you more lies _____ than the cross - ties on the
lis - ten to me. _____ Never place your af -

Duet Part (Student plays one octave higher than written.)

Moderately slow

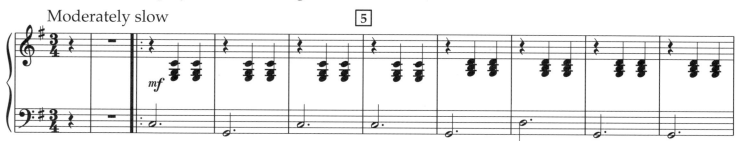

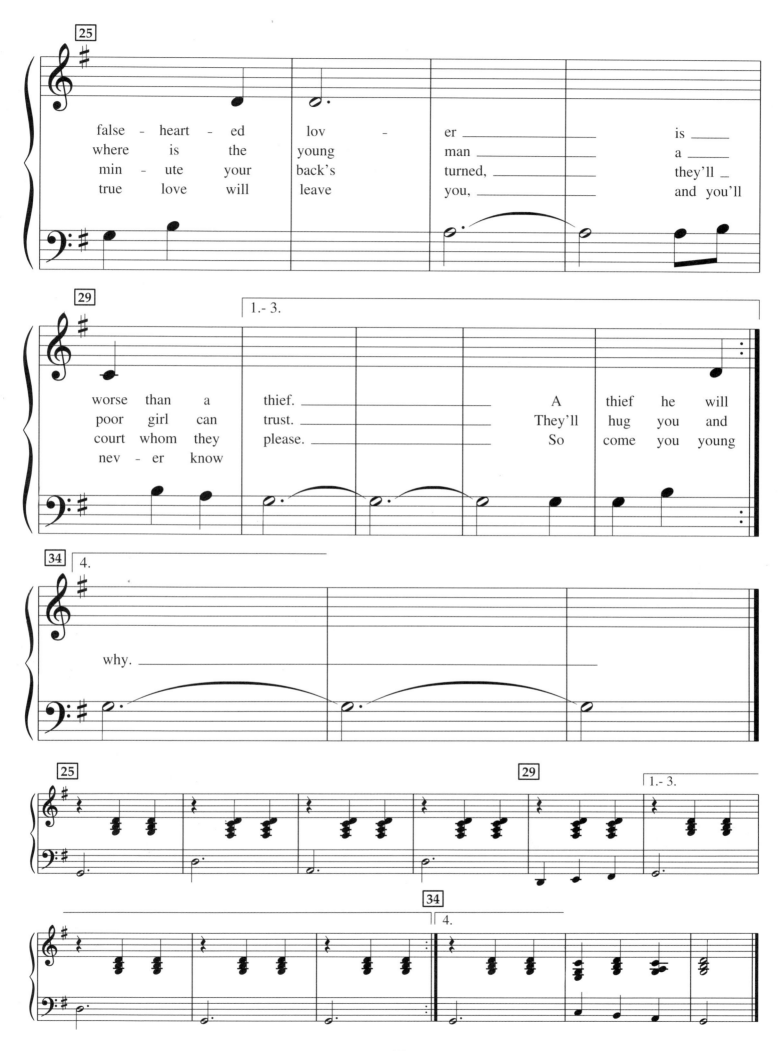

Hush, Little Baby

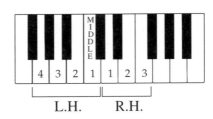

Gently

Carolina Folk Lullaby

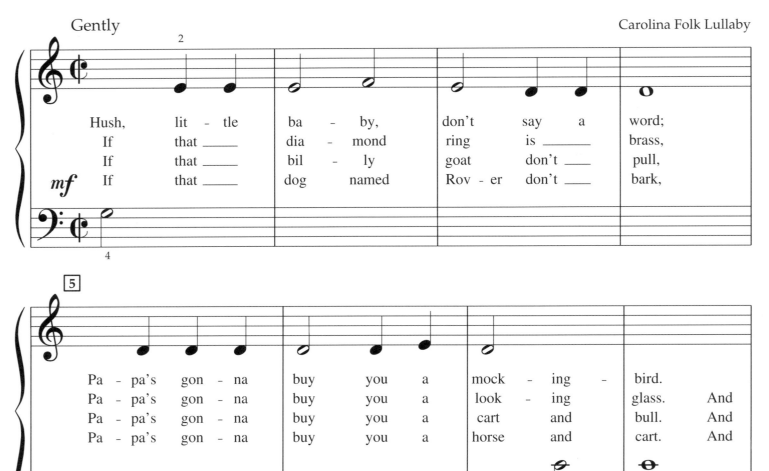

Hush, lit - tle ba - by, don't say a word;
If that _____ dia - mond ring is _____ brass,
If that _____ bil - ly goat don't _____ pull,
If that _____ dog named Rov - er don't _____ bark,

Pa - pa's gon - na buy you a mock - ing - bird.
Pa - pa's gon - na buy you a look - ing glass. And
Pa - pa's gon - na buy you a cart and bull. And
Pa - pa's gon - na buy you a horse and cart. And

Duet Part (Student plays one octave higher than written.)

Gently

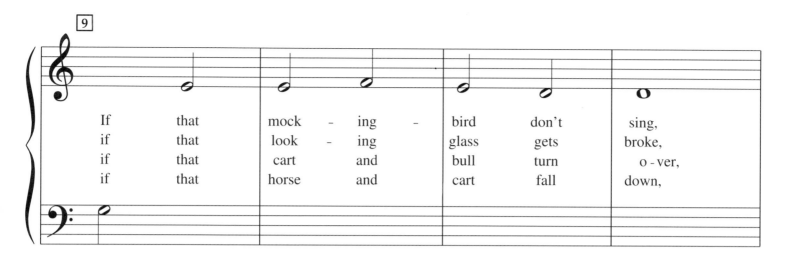

If that mock - ing - bird don't sing,
if that look - ing glass gets broke,
if that cart and bull turn o - ver,
if that horse and cart fall down,

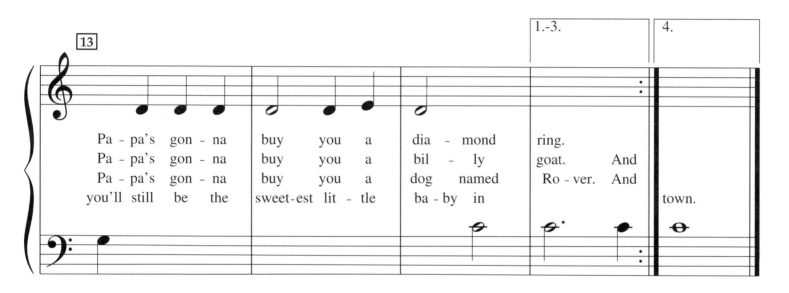

1.-3. 4.

Pa - pa's gon - na buy you a dia - mond ring.
Pa - pa's gon - na buy you a bil - ly goat. And
Pa - pa's gon - na buy you a dog named Ro - ver. And
you'll still be the sweet-est lit - tle ba - by in town.

1.-3. 4.

If You're Happy and You Know It

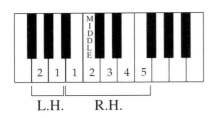

Traditional American Game Song

Playfully

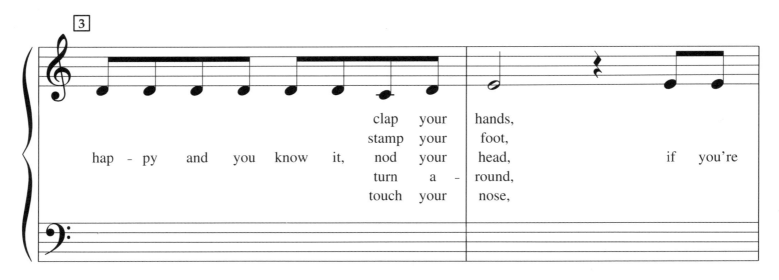

Duet Part (Student plays one octave higher than written.)

Playfully

(Clap clap)

hap - py   and   you   know   it,   then   your | face   will   sure - ly   show   it,   if   you're

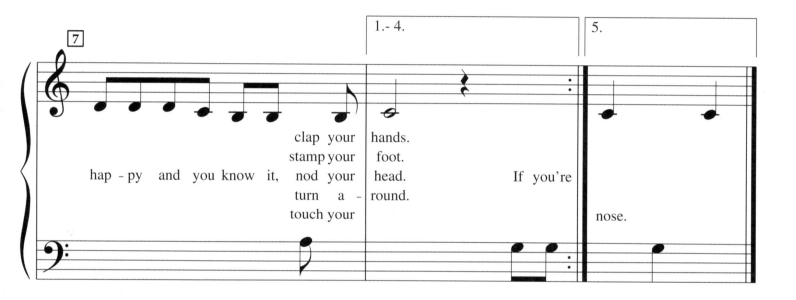

1.- 4.

5.

clap your | hands.
stamp your | foot.
hap - py   and   you know it,   nod your | head.   If   you're
turn a - | round.
touch your | nose.

The Old Gray Mare

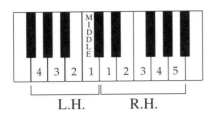

Tennessee Folksong

With spirit

Oh, the Old Gray Mare, she ain't what she used to be, ain't what she used to be,

ain't what she used to be. The Old Gray Mare, she ain't what she used to be

Duet Part (Student plays one octave higher than written.)

With spirit

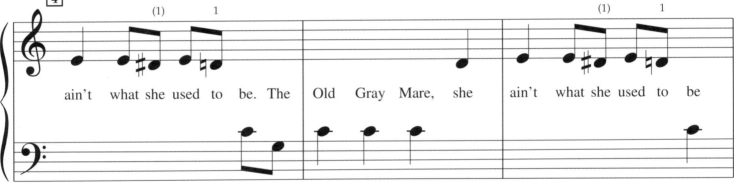

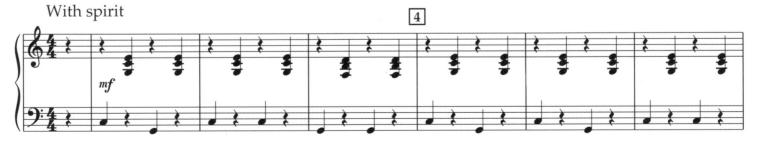

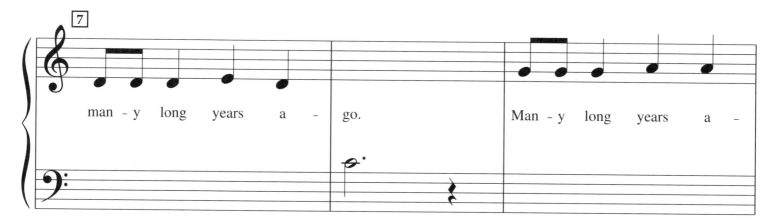

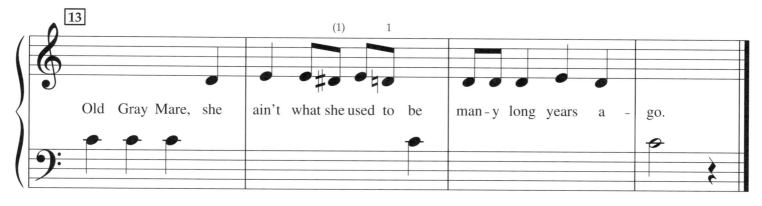

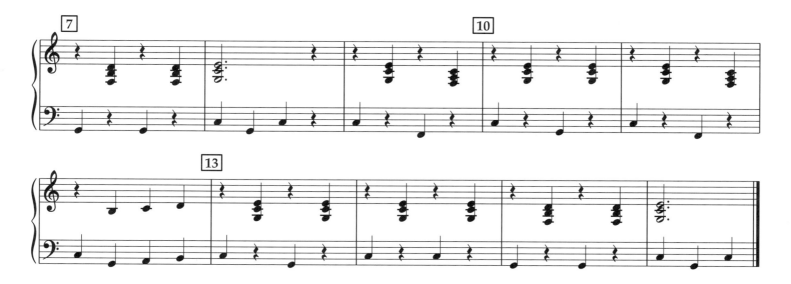

Row, Row, Row Your Boat

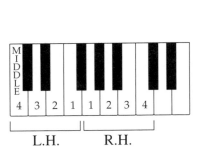

L.H.   R.H.

American Folk Round

With a rocking motion

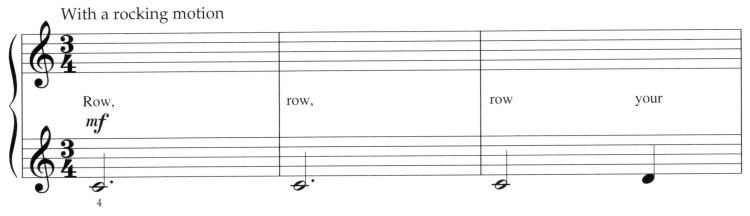

Row,   row,   row   your

boat,   gen - tly   down   the

Duet Part (Student plays one octave higher than written.)

With a rocking motion

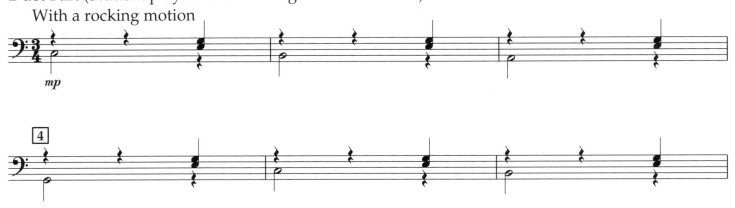

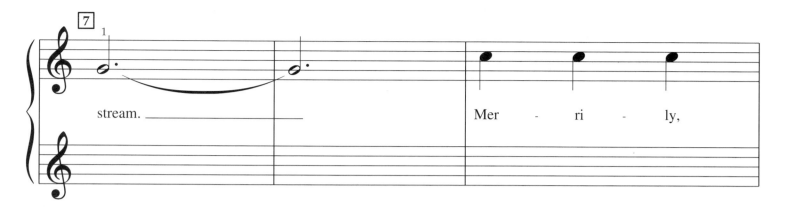

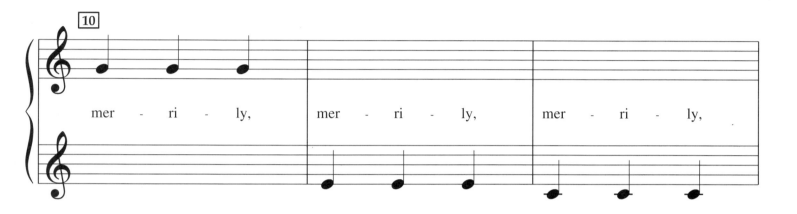

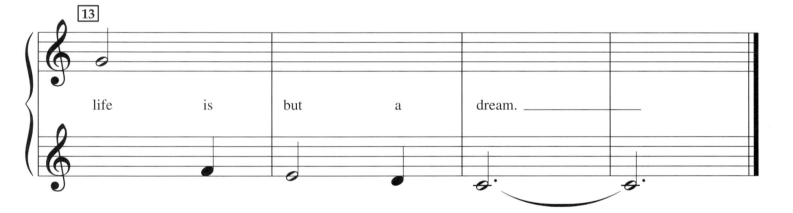

There's a Hole in the Bottom of the Sea

Traditional Children's Song

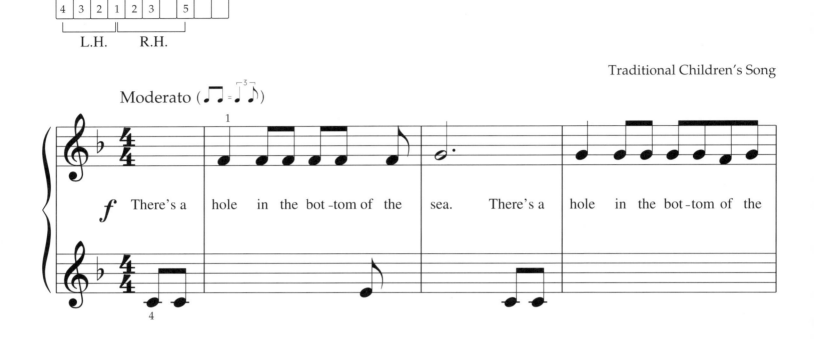

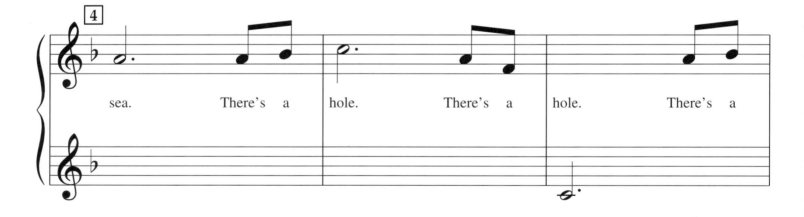

Duet Part (Student plays one octave higher than written.)

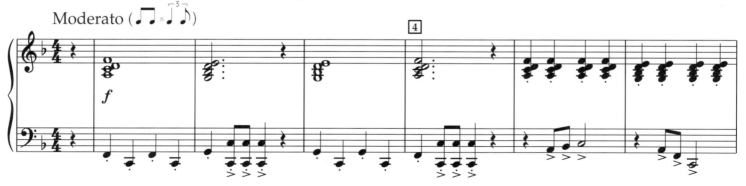

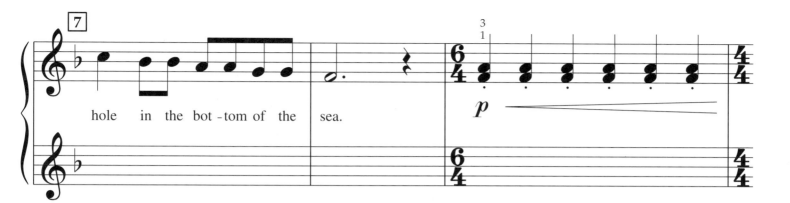

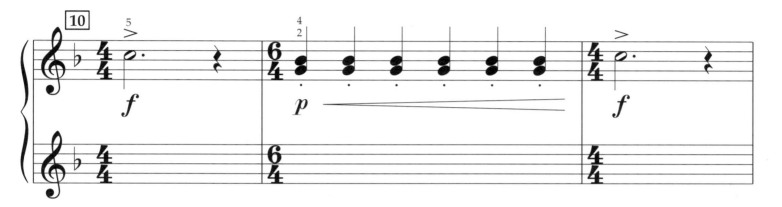

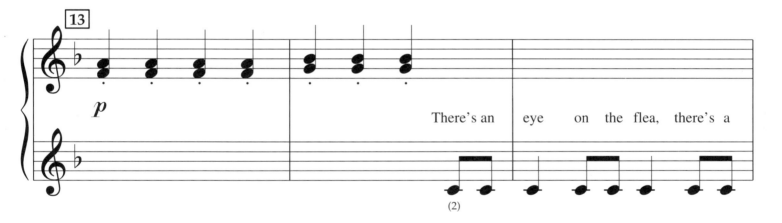

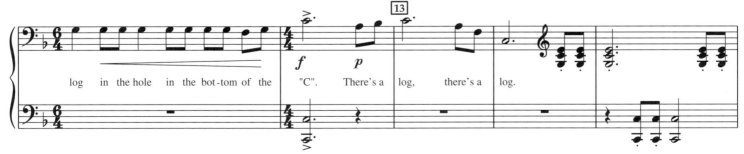

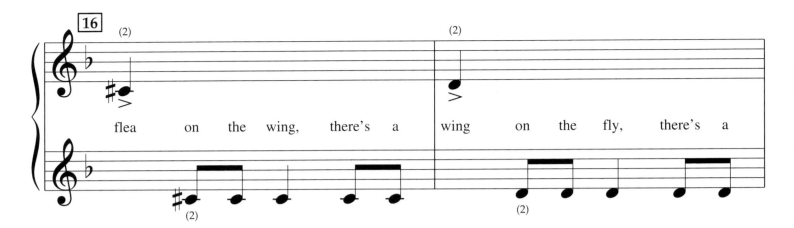

flea on the wing, there's a wing on the fly, there's a

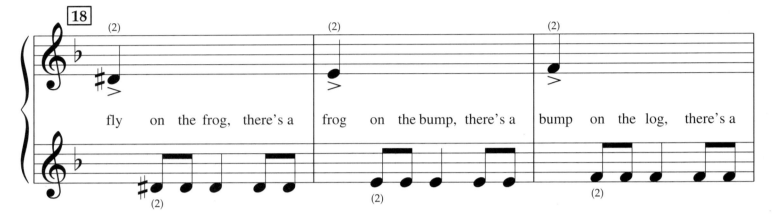

fly on the frog, there's a frog on the bump, there's a bump on the log, there's a

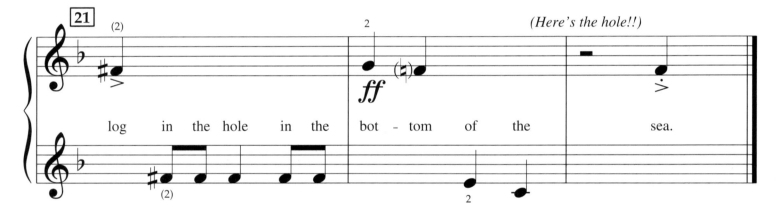

(Here's the hole!!)

log in the hole in the bot - tom of the sea.

When the Saints Go Marching In

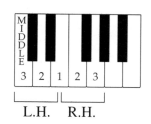

Words by Katherine E. Purvis
Music by James M. Black

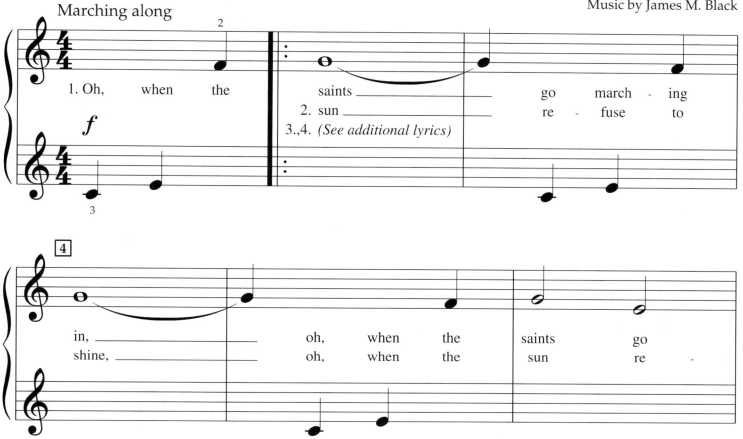

Duet Part (Student plays one octave higher than written.)

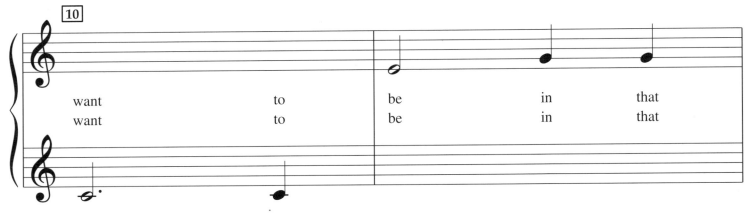

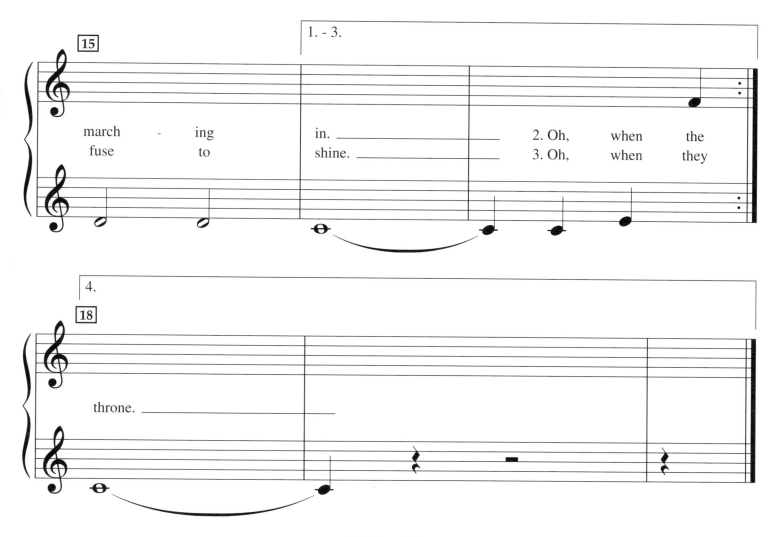

Additional Lyrics

3. Oh, when they crown Him Lord of all,
   Oh, when they crown Him Lord of all;
   Oh Lord, I want to be in that number
   When they crown Him Lord of All.

4. Oh, when they gather 'round the throne,
   Oh, when they gather 'round the throne;
   Oh Lord, I want to be in that number
   When they gather 'round the throne.

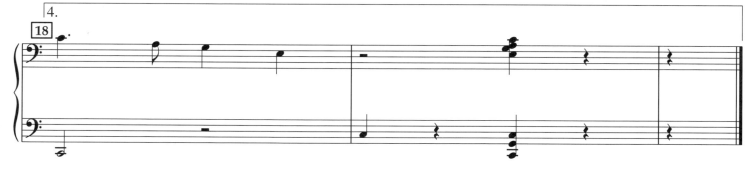

PLAYING PIANO
HAS NEVER BEEN EASIER!

5-Finger Piano Collections from Hal Leonard

BEATLES FAVORITES

8 songs, including: All My Loving • All You Need Is Love • Here Comes the Sun • Michelle • and more.
00310369 ....$7.95

BROADWAY SONGS FOR KIDS

8 songs, including: Castle On A Cloud • Do- Re- Mi • I Won't Grow Up • Tomorrow • and more.
00310067 ....$6.95

CARTOON FUN

7 fun favorites, including: Meet The Flintstones • The Jetsons • Popeye The Sailor Man • Duck Tales • and more.
00292064 ....$6.95

CHILDREN'S CHOICE

8 fun favorites, including: The Addams Family Theme • Peter Cottontail • Supercalifragilisticexpiali-docious • Winnie The Pooh • Won't You Be My Neighbor? • and more.
00310091...............................$6.95

DISNEY MOVIE FUN

8 classics, including: Beauty And The Beast • When You Wish Upon A Star • Whistle While You Work • and more.
00292067...............................$6.95

EENSY WEENSY SPIDER & OTHER NURSERY RHYME FAVORITES

12 classics, including the title song and: Hickory Dickory Dock • Humpty Dumpty • Jack and Jill • Pop Goes the Weasel • and more.
00310465 ....$7.95

FAVORITE HYMNS

10 hymns: Amazing Grace • Fairest Lord Jesus • I Love to Tell the Story • Standing on the Promises • Were You There • and more.
00310121 ....$5.95

THE LION KING

5 songs from the Disney hit: Can You Feel The Love Tonight • Circle Of Life • Hakuna Matata • I Just Can't Wait To Be King • and more.
00292062...............................$7.95

MY FAVORITE THINGS

Arr. by Mac Huff
Includes: Chim Chim Cheree • Do-Re-Mi • Edelweiss • It's A Small World • and more.
00240258 ....$6.95

OUR FAVORITE FOLKSONGS

9 songs, including: Down in the Valley • Oh! Susanna • Yankee Doodle • and more.
00310068 ....$5.95

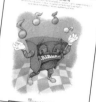

SUPER SILLY SONGS

Includes: Be Kind to Your Web-Footed Friends • Little Bunny Foo Foo • The Man on the Flying Trapeze • Who Threw the Overalls in Mrs. Murphy's Chowder? • more.
00310136 ....$6.95

TV TIME

8 great show themes, including: The Brady Bunch • The Munster's Theme • Star Trek – The Next Generation • and more.
00292069 ....$6.95

FOR MORE INFORMATION, SEE YOUR LOCAL MUSIC DEALER,
OR WRITE TO:

HAL•LEONARD®
CORPORATION
7777 W. BLUEMOUND RD. P.O. BOX 13819 MILWAUKEE, WI 53213